# Faerie Gold

A Guide for
Teachers and Students

## Classics for Young Readers

*Sir Gibbie* by George Macdonald
*Sir Gibbie: A Guide for Teachers and Students*
*Hans Brinker* by Mary Mapes Dodge
*Hans Brinker: A Guide for Teachers and Students*
*A Little Princess* by Frances Hodgson Burnett
*A Little Princess: A Guide for Teachers and Students*
*Black Beauty* by Anna Sewell
*Black Beauty: A Guide for Teachers and Students*
*Robinson Crusoe* by Daniel Defoe
*Robinson Crusoe: A Guide for Teachers and Students*
*Little Women* by Louisa May Alcott
*Little Women: A Guide for Teachers and Students*
*Faerie Gold: Treasures from the Lands of Enchantment*
*Faerie Gold: A Guide for Teachers and Students*

# Faerie Gold

A Guide for
Teachers and Students

Ranelda Mack Hunsicker

P&R
P U B L I S H I N G
P.O. BOX 817 • PHILLIPSBURG • NEW JERSEY 08865-0817

*Design by Tobias Design*
*Typesetting by Dawn Premako*

Printed in the United States of America

**Library of Congress Cataloging-in-Publication Data**

Hunsicker, Ranelda Mack, 1953–
Faerie gold : a guide for teachers and students / Ranelda Mack Hunsicker.
p. cm. — (Classics for young readers)
ISBN 0-87552-741-8
1. Fairy tales—Study and teaching. 2. Oral reading. I. Title. II. Series.

LB1575.H85 2004
372.64—dc22

2004057326

# Contents

# To Parents and Teachers . . .

Exploring fairytales is an adventure like no other. As brilliant fantasy writer J. R. R. Tolkien observes, "The realm of fairy story is wide and deep and high and filled with many things: all manner of beasts and birds are found there; shoreless seas and stars uncounted; beauty that is an enchantment, and an everpresent peril; both joy and sorrow as sharp as swords." This emotionally charged land of wonder can produce profound thoughts and feelings that are difficult, if not impossible, to express. Tolkien writes, "In that realm a man may, perhaps, count himself fortunate to have wandered, but its very richness and strangeness tie the tongue of a traveler who would report them. And while he is there it is dangerous for him to ask too many questions, lest the gates should be shut and the keys be lost."

This study guide attempts to offer some direction for exploring the land of Faerie without shattering its enchantment. Instead of the usual emphasis on reading comprehension questions, readers are encouraged to respond to stories in personal ways, expressing their sense of wonder in a variety of creative activities.

Each story in the *Faerie Gold* anthology is accompanied by the following study guide sections:

**Unlocking Word Treasures.** Since the *Faerie Gold* anthology contains stories of widely differing reading levels, a look at the vocabulary section provides a quick way to decide if a story is best as a read-aloud selection or can be enjoyed as an independent reading assignment. Reluctant readers may benefit by studying the vocabulary lists before reading each story. This provides them with greater reading confidence and less distraction from the story content. More gifted readers will know many of the vocabulary words or will deduce their meaning from the text itself. For definitions of vocabulary, consult *Webster's New Collegiate Dictionary.*

**Sharing the Wonder.** The whole family or class can enjoy these classic stories together. Whenever possible, adults and young readers should take turns reading pages or chapters aloud. Then provide an opportunity to respond to the story. Encourage self-expression while remembering Tolkien's warning against asking too many questions. Perhaps a story will remind readers of a musical composition or work of art with the same mood. It may suggest comparisons with other fantasy tales. It may trigger a debate about good and evil, motives and meaning. It may spark curiosity about the kind of person who created the story. Hopefully it will lead to:

**Finding Your Own Faerie Gold**. Through personal artwork, drama and writing, readers can enter the realm of Faerie in an even deeper way. Suggested activities are designed to help students move from enjoying and understanding the story to responding at a more personal level, a key element in internalizing and applying truth.

**Literary Terms.** Some students using this study guide are ready for an introduction to literary terms. In addition to providing definitions and examples of some important terms, the discussion questions and creative exercises provide opportunities to gain experience in using the language of literature.

Chapter 1

# LITTLE DAYLIGHT

by George MacDonald

## Part 1: Unlocking Word Treasures

*Here are some words to add to your vocabulary treasure chest. Look up the meanings of those you don't know in a dictionary.*

| | | |
|---|---|---|
| weathercock | noblemen | jubilation |
| generation | mortals | vengeance |
| christening | plague | archbishop |
| axle | bestow | prospect |
| wax and wane | crone | propriety |
| duration | almanac | crescent |
| rustic | glade | massacre |
| inhabit | nightingale | thatched |
| entranced | scheming | consequence |
| contrive | tinderbox | cordial |

## Part 2: Sharing the Wonder

1. The author says that a palace must have a wood near it. Why is a wood necessary? Can you think of other fairy tales where a wood is important to the story?
2. If Little Daylight lived at your house, how would life change?
3. What disguises were used in this story? What people and things were not what they appeared?

4. What kind of music do you think Little Daylight danced to in the glade?
5. If you could be someone in this story, who would you choose to be?

*VIEWPOINT:* Like a photographer choosing the right angle and distance from which to take a picture, a writer chooses a point of view in telling a story. The writer may tell the story from what we could call "a God's eye view" or an "all-knowing" perspective; this allows readers to see things from many different angles. More often, writers choose to tell their stories from the viewpoint of one or two main characters.

## Part 3: Finding Your Own Faerie Gold

**Brainstorm:** Think of some words that describe the swamp fairy. What was she like? What was her main goal? What strategies did the swamp fairy use? Who interfered with her goal? How might she have felt toward them? In what ways did she defeat her own evil plans?

**Go for the Gold!** (Choose one.)

- Tell the story of "Little Daylight" from the *viewpoint* of the swamp fairy. If she wrote about what happened, what would she say?
- The swamp fairy is forced to move in with the motherly fairy in the rustic cottage. Tell the story of what happens.
- Write a letter to parents with advice about what to do about fairy gifts their children receive.

Chapter 2

# THE FAIRY'S NEW YEAR GIFT

by Emilie Poulsson

## Part 1: Unlocking Word Treasures

One of the fascinating things about words is how many different ways they can be used. Their meanings can change like magic, depending on how they are put into a sentence or what we want them to say. For example, the word *wonder* can simply mean that we want to know more about something, that we are curious or in doubt. *Wonder* can also mean that something causes us amazement and delight, makes us awestruck.

In "The Fairy's New Year Gift," there are four other words that can have very different meanings than they do in this story. Write down two meanings for each of the following four words (including the meaning of each word as it is used in the story).

leaf
fast
fair
spray

## Part 2: Sharing the Wonder

1. This story uses a *metaphor* to help us understand the importance of our daily choices. What is that metaphor?
2. In what ways is your life like a book?

3. Is there any way to erase mistakes in your life book? (Before you answer, read Acts 3:19, Isaiah 44:22, and Psalm 51:1–12.)
4. Do you know someone whose life book is especially beautiful and inspiring to look at? Describe him or her.

METAPHOR: Are you telling a lie when you say that something is what it is not? The answer is yes, *unless* you are using a metaphor. This kind of word magic is a comparison between two things that do not seem to be alike. A metaphor connects an object, place, or event to something we would not normally associate with it. By doing this, writers can help us see things in fresh new ways. For example, Jesus used a metaphor when He told His disciples, "You are the salt of the earth." He did not mean they would be turned into actual salt, but He wanted them to realize something about them was like salt.

## Part 3: Finding Your Own Faerie Gold

**Brainstorm:** If you could make a book to picture the past week of your life, what would it look like? Would it be big or little? What would its cover look like? Would its pages be made of white or colored paper? What kinds of pictures would be on each of its daily pages? How would the pages be fastened together—with yarn or ribbon, staples, glue? What things have happened in the past week that might be recorded in your book?

**Go for the Gold!** (Choose one.)

- Make a book that illustrates the past week of your life. Be as honest as you can about how each page looks. Portray each day in words and pictures.

- Make a blank book to fill in each day during the next week. At the end of each day think about the choices you made, the things you said and did, and how you can record them on the page. Then think about how to make the next day's page more beautiful. Add your favorite Scripture verses.

## Chapter 3

# PRINCE CHERRY

by Dinah Mulock Craik

### Part 1: Unlocking Word Treasures

*Add these words to your vocabulary treasure chest by writing a short definition for each one.*

| | | |
|---|---|---|
| monarch | hutch | garland |
| external | prick | amend |
| indulge | accustomed | dispute |
| injustice | contradict | impulses |
| irons | gluttony | revenge |
| brutality | transform | transport |
| submission | viceroy | tainted |
| reform | menagerie | ferocious |
| adorn | conscience | slew |
| hermit | peasant | mutual |
| frugal | vainly | blameless |

## Part 2: Sharing the Wonder

1. In *fantasy* stories, often a person, animal, or object changes into something else. How many of these transformations, or changes, can you find in "Prince Cherry"?
2. The fairy Candide compared Prince Cherry to a wolf, a serpent, and a bull. In what ways was he like these three animals?
3. Sometimes truth is stranger than fiction. In the Bible you'll find the story of a real king who had an experience like Prince Cherry. Turn to the fourth chapter of the Old Testament book of Daniel for this amazing story.

FANTASY: When writers create fantasy stories, they mix things from the world of make-believe with things from the world of reality. Things happen that could never happen in our everyday lives, but if the writer does a good job these fantastic things seem believable while we are reading the story. It is as if the writer has created a new world and we step into it for a while.

## Part 3: Finding Your Own Faerie Gold

**Brainstorm:** Make a list of words that you connect with certain animals. For example, the word *lion* makes many people think of strength or courage. If you began to look like the animals you behave most like, which animals would they be? If you could change for a while into another creature, which would you choose?

**Go for the Gold!** (Choose one.)

- Write your own short fairy tale in which Candide visits you and turns you into a fantasy creature. Be sure to include:

1. Her reason for doing this,
2. what it was like to live in a different body, and
3. how you got back to your true form.

- Write one or two pages in which you compare "Prince Cherry" to three other fantasy stories where people change into animal-like creatures. How are the stories alike? How are they different?

Chapter 4

# KENNETH AND THE CARP

by Edith Nesbit

## Part 1: Unlocking Word Treasures

*Sometimes it helps to put new words you are learning into groups, based on something they have in common. After you're sure what each of the following words means, sort them into these groups: JEWELS, CLOTHES, BUILDINGS, WATER.*

| | | |
|---|---|---|
| carp | amethyst | moat |
| halibut | cloak | moorings |
| muslin | topaz | punt |
| train | mariner | attic |
| parlor | sash | men-o'war |
| satin | dagger | eel |
| flannel | gills | veil |

## Part 2: Sharing the Wonder

1. "Kenneth and the Carp" doesn't seem to be a fairytale until we reach the middle. What words start the magic? Do you think Kenneth thought about these words before he said them? Have you ever said something similar without thinking what might happen if your words came true?
2. How would this story be different if Edith Nesbit had started it at the point where Alison borrowed her sister's jewelry without permission? Would the story be better or worse? Why? How would the story change if it began as Kenneth fell into the water?
3. What gave Kenneth the courage to do something he knew would hurt badly? What did he have to think about instead of the hook? What can you learn from him about facing something difficult? For another example of how to go on when you feel like giving up, read Hebrews 12:1–2. What did Kenneth and Jesus have in common?

PLOT: Writers create stories by figuring out how to tell readers about a series of events in an order that leads toward solution of a problem. A story plot has: a *beginning*, where the problem or conflict is introduced; a *middle*, where readers learn more about the main characters and the challenges they face; and an *ending*, where the suspense about how the problem will be solved reaches a high point and the conclusion is presented. To make a story interesting and logical, writers must be careful about the order or sequence in which they tell each event.

## Part 3: Finding Your Own Faerie Gold

**Brainstorm:** Edith Nesbit says that the first duty, or job, of a storyteller is to tell things in their proper order. Write each of the main events in "Kenneth and the Carp" on a 3"x5" index card, using complete sentences. Do not number these cards in any way.

**Go for the Gold!** Shuffle the story cards you just made so they are in no particular order. Now give them to a friend or family member who hasn't read "Kenneth and the Carp." Ask them to put the cards in the best order they can to make a story. When they are finished, tell them the story in your own words and let them see how close they came to Edith Nesbit's *plot*.

**Chapter 5**

# THE SKIPPING SHOES

by Louisa May Alcott

## Part 1: Unlocking Word Treasures

This story is full of busy, active words. We call these words *verbs*. By choosing the best verbs for each of their sentences, writers can help readers see more clearly what is happening. Make a list of all the verbs Louisa May Alcott used to describe how Kitty's shoes carried her from one place to another. Think about how you can use more interesting verbs when you speak and write.

## Part 2: Sharing the Wonder

1. Kitty knew the story of "The Seven-League Boots." Do you? What other stories can you think of that have magical shoes?
2. In what way did Louisa May Alcott use *personification* in "The Skipping Shoes"?
3. At what point did Kitty decide to be good without the help of her shoes? Why do you think she made this decision?
4. What is the difference between obeying because you must and obeying because you choose to? (Colossians 3:1–17; Ephesians 5:1; 6:7; Romans 6:16–17)

PERSONIFICATION: This may look like a very difficult word, but it really isn't once you notice its most important part—*person*. When writers and storytellers use personification, they give something that isn't human some abilities that only humans have. In other words, they make a thing act like a person.

## Part 3: Finding Your Own Faerie Gold

**Brainstorm:** Imagine that it is your birthday and one of your gifts is a new piece of clothing. Picture in your mind what this gift looks like. Now imagine that this piece of clothing has some human qualities. What would it do, think or say?

**Go for the Gold!** (Choose one.)

- Write a one- or two-page story in which something you are wearing comes to life.
- Write a one-page letter to yourself from something you are wearing. Let this piece of clothing, shoes, or jewelry talk to you like a person.

## Chapter 6

# THE ENCHANTED NECKLACE

by Annie Fellows Johnston

### Part 1: Unlocking Word Treasures

*Here are some words to add to your vocabulary treasure chest. Once you're sure what each word means, you're ready to use it in a sentence. Can you use all these words in seven clear, sensible sentences? (Look to see how the starred words are used in the story, since they can have very different meanings.)*

| | | |
|---|---|---|
| maiden | flax | *charger |
| bugle | courier | realm |
| *ball | *dame | garb |
| toil | spindle | distaff |
| wreath | shrivel | *tow |
| clasp | texture | daffodil |
| bestow | haughty | sacrifice |
| vain | destiny | gossamer |
| ermine | | |

### Part 2: Sharing the Wonder

1. There are some important *symbols* in this story. They are: Olga's dress of tow, the old flax spinner's drops of blood, the enchanted necklace, and the flowers that bloomed at the castle gate. What ideas do you think each of these symbols represents?

2. What made Olga forgetful about some very important things?
3. Special Challenge: Sometimes numbers are symbols of ideas. To Jews and Christians, seven is a very special number because on the seventh day of creation the world was complete and God rested. The number seven is a symbol for things that are complete or perfect. Is it important that Olga's necklace had exactly "seventy times seven" beads? (Hint: Look at Matthew 18:21–22.)

SYMBOL: When we use numbers, we are using symbols that stand for a certain quantity or amount of something. When we use letters, we are using symbols that stand for certain sounds. When we use words, we are using symbols that represent certain ideas. When a writer or speaker wants to present an idea that is difficult to describe, he may use a concrete thing as a symbol of this idea. For example: in the United States, the eagle is a symbol of our nation's freedom and strength; for Christians, the anchor is a symbol of unchanging, immovable hope; and in many cultures the circle is a symbol of eternity or unending time.

## Part 3: Finding Your Own Faerie Gold

**Brainstorm:** In five minutes, see how many story book symbols you can list. When you are through making your list, write down next to each symbol what it represents. (Example: apple, temptation/danger, "Snow White")

**Go for the Gold!** (Choose one.)

- Choose your favorite symbol from the list you just made. Make a poster about this symbol and its meaning. You can use your own drawings, stickers, and pictures from old magazines (with permission!) to illustrate what the symbol means to you.

- Create a full-page advertisement (like those you see in magazines) for the enchanted necklace. Use pictures and words to describe what it can do and why someone would want it. What company would offer the necklace? (You can make up a company name.) What would people pay for the necklace? (Or would it take something besides money to get it?) Who should they contact if they want more information?

## Chapter 7

# THE GOLD-BEARDED MAN

by Andrew Lang

### Part 1: Unlocking Word Treasures

*Write a short definition for each of the following words.*

| | | |
|---|---|---|
| coffin | spite | scheme |
| flask | captive | earnestly |
| twilight | implore | proverb |
| rushes (noun) | discharge | steward |
| barley | council | brook |
| prophet | vow | chamber |
| swaddling | lute | zither |

## Part 2: Sharing the Wonder

1. Make a list of the main things that happened to the prince in "The Gold-Bearded Man." Which things happened to him because of what someone else did? Which things happened because of what the prince did?
2. What was the main cause of the prince's good fortune?
3. A proverb is repeated several times in this story: "Mountain and mountain can never meet, but one living creature can always come across another." What are some other ways we could say the same thing?
4. Can you think of any teachings in the Bible that this story illustrates? (Hints: Matthew 5:7; Galatians 6:7-10; Proverbs 19:17; Luke 6:38.)

CAUSE AND EFFECT: In a story it is important for us to see how one thing leads to another, how a word or action causes a certain result or consequence. Even when magical things take place, we want to be able to look back in the story to what someone did and say to ourselves, "Oh, yes, because she did that, now this is happening." This makes the story believable.

## Part 3: Finding Your Own Faerie Gold

**Brainstorm:** What if the prince had not released the gold-bearded man from his cage? What if the prince had not run away from home after releasing the gold-bearded man? What if the prince had killed and eaten the wood pigeon? What if the prince had met two good soldiers instead two bad ones? What if the prince had tried to get even with the two bad soldiers instead of outsmarting them? How would different choices change the rest of the story?

**Go for the Gold!** (Choose one.)

- Change a main event in "The Gold-Bearded Man." Now write a new ending for the story based on the event you have changed. Be sure the ending shows how the event you changed causes different consequences.
- Turn "The Gold-Bearded Man" into a newspaper article. Remember to include the main ingredients of a news story, the Five Ws: **who** (the main characters), **what** (the main events), **when** (the time of the main events), **where** (the place where the events happen), and **why** (the causes of the events).

## Chapter 8

# THE PRINCESS OF THE GOLDEN CASTLE

by Katherine Pyle

### Part 1: Unlocking Word Treasures

*Check in the dictionary to be sure you know what these words mean. Next to each word, write down what part of speech it is (noun, verb, adjective, adverb) and if it can be used in two very different ways.*

| | | |
|---|---|---|
| solemn | ajar | porridge |
| cease | gruel | withered |
| counterpane | dome | triumphantly |
| deed | arched | emerald |

| thrust | nimbly | goblet |
|---|---|---|
| heed | courtier | coverlet |

## Part 2: Sharing the Wonder

1. When we read or hear a story in which the hero has to figure out which is the right door, box, or path, we expect the storyteller to give some clues to help the hero make the choice. In this story, there is only one clue. What is it? Why do you think Teddy ignored it for so long?
2. If Teddy had paid better attention to the fairy's clue, could he have rescued the princess on his first try? Why or why not?
3. There is more than one kind of *conflict* in this story. Some of the conflict came from outside Teddy and some came from inside. What were these conflicts? What challenges did Teddy face and how did he solve them?
4. How would this story be different if Teddy had had a television in his room?

CONFLICT: When there is a struggle between opponents, there is conflict. This conflict can be between a person and:

- other people
- animals
- nature or weather (like a mountain or storm)
- society (groups of people who share certain beliefs)
- oneself

The conflict in a story makes it interesting because we wonder what will happen next and who will win. In fact, without some kind of conflict, there is no story.

## Part 3: Finding Your Own Faerie Gold

**Brainstorm:** Look at several fairy tale picture books to see how artists illustrate what happens in the story. If you don't have any, visit the library and check out a few. Then think about how "The Princess of the Golden Castle" could be made into a picture book. How many pictures would the story need? What would each picture show?

**Go for the Gold!** (Choose one.)

- Draw one of the illustrations this story needs. Do your best to make it match the information given in the story, but use your imagination to add details the writer didn't give. One example of a detail you might need to add is clothing for Teddy.
- If you are fond of drawing, make a complete picture book of "The Princess of the Golden Castle." Then share your drawings and the story with someone.

**Chapter 9**

# THE GATE OF THE GIANT SCISSORS

by Annie Fellows Johnston

## Part 1: Unlocking Word Treasures

*When we read or listen to a story, we don't have to know all the words in it to understand most of what happens. But knowing all the words makes the story even better! How many of these words from "The Gate of the Giant Scissors" do you already know? Which ones can you add to your word treasure chest by looking them up in the dictionary?*

| | | |
|---|---|---|
| tournament | armor | plume |
| scorn | mantle | jester |
| girdle | moor | cowardly |
| strand | brow | filmy |
| domain | snare | perseverance |
| seize | extend | thicket |
| onslaught | chasm | wrath |
| gnash | millstone | spied |
| dungeon | clammy | clutch |
| thrust | fiendish | dismal |
| gratitude | shutter | glimmer |
| tempest | bewilderment | orchard |
| peasant | idleness | stalk |
| fleece | merchant | herald |
| potentate | wring | combat |
| wily | swoop | rent (as in, *tear*) |
| valor | gable | valiant |
| portal | | |

## Part 2: Sharing the Wonder

1. What serious mistake did the king make in judging his seven sons? (Hint: 1 Samuel 16:7)
2. Even though the king was making fun of his son when he gave him the scissors, this gift turned out to be good for Ethelried. What helped to turn this cruel gift into a blessing?

3. Read the Old Testament story of David and Goliath (1 Samuel 17). In what ways is Ethelried's story like this Bible story?

RHYME: When writers repeat vowel sounds in the words they use, they are making rhymes. For example, Dr. Seuss used many rhymes in his books and book titles, like *The Cat in the Hat*. The words of songs often contain rhymes, and so do many poems. In poetry, most often the rhymes are found at the end of a verse-line. For example:

> The world is so full of a number of things,
> I'm sure we should all be as happy as kings.
> —Robert Louis Stevenson

Sometimes writers rhyme every other line in their poems. There can also be words that rhyme within the line, and this is called internal rhyme.

## Part 3: Finding Your Own Faerie Gold

**Brainstorm:** In "The Gate of the Giant Scissors" we are told, "the art of rhyming had been neglected in his [Ethelried's] early education." As a result, he had a hard time thinking up *rhymes* to make the magic scissors work. How good are you at creating rhymes? In three minutes, see how many rhymes you can think of to put the scissors to work.

**Go for the Gold!** (Choose one.)

Write a four- to eight-line rhyming poem about:

- Frog-eye Fearsome
- Ethelried
- the peasant farmer
- the captive princess

Chapter 10

# THE GREEDY SHEPHERD

by Frances Browne

## Part 1: Unlocking Word Treasures

*Look to see how the starred words are used in the story before writing down their definitions.*

| | | |
|---|---|---|
| cottage | heath | profit |
| agreeable | sycamore | *pipe |
| *crook | *plain | ancient |
| shears | persuade | dispute |
| stray | boast | primrose |
| divert | crimson | despise |
| poverty | advice | moorlands |
| *cleft | violets | holly |
| employment | *stout | fortune |
| devour | | |

## Part 2: Sharing the Wonder

1. In an *allegory,* the story characters often have names that fit the way they act or speak. How do the names of the two shepherds in this story fit them?
2. "The Ugly Duckling" is a famous fairy tale allegory that you may have heard. As you probably remember, everyone made fun of the Ugly Duckling because he looked so different than the rest of the baby ducks. As he grew up, it became clear he looked dif-

ferent because he was a swan. When we think about this story, we can find another story hiding in its background—a story about how people who seem odd or unlikable may turn out to be beautiful outside and/or inside.

3. As you think about the tale of "The Greedy Shepherd," what might it be about besides just what happened to two shepherds?
4. Have you ever known someone who treated people the way Clutch treated his sheep? What are some ways we can be more like Kind than like Clutch?

ALLEGORY: Almost any kind of story or poem can be written in the form of an allegory. In an allegory, the characters, location, and events have double meanings—the one we see easily and the one we discover when we think about the story for a while. By using certain symbols or word pictures throughout the whole story, the allegory shows us some truth about life. Sometimes Jesus told stories that were allegories, like His story of the prodigal son (Luke 15:11-31).

## Part 3: Finding Your Own Faerie Gold

**Brainstorm:** Think about how you could rewrite "The Greedy Shepherd" by changing an important part of it. What would happen if you changed the characters' names? their occupation? the place where the story happens? the person they met high in the mountains? How does changing one thing bring about other changes in the story?

**Go for the Gold!** (Choose one.)

Rewrite "The Greedy Shepherd" by changing:

- The names Clutch and Kind to Coward and Courageous

- Clutch and Kind into gardeners
- The ancient man in the mountains into a troll
- The mountains into a cave

When you are finished, see if your story is an allegory. If it is, what important truth does it teach through word pictures?

Chapter 11

# FLORA'S BIRTHDAY PARTY

by Christina Rossetti

## Part 1: Unlocking Word Treasures

*Some words that people once used regularly are scarcely ever used today. This story has some old-fashioned words in it that are listed below. Once you know what these words mean, see if you can find a modern word to replace them.*

| | | |
|---|---|---|
| sugarplums | harmonium | looking-glass |
| ottoman | morsel | greengages |
| angelica | hued | frock |
| recollection | dainties | |

You may also need to add the following words to your vocabulary before reading "Flora's Birthday Party."

| | | |
|---|---|---|
| pincushion | accompanied | elegant |
| superior | soothing | regretful |
| bawl | discord | yew |
| sheer | mulberries | sulk |

sullen
convenience
expand
mope
jostle
patience
conclude
tormentor
maximum
plait
dignity
enclose
uniformly
chrysolite
illuminate
trace
grimace
amethyst
massive
launch
laurel

provoking
disadvantage
contract
flushed
tolerance
overtake
strain
exasperated
crimp
philosopher
sympathy
tenacity
varied
sapphire
abundance
pantry
amber
hailstone
heave
fleet
nestle

lag
telescope
bulge
scudded
forbearance
interval
swerve
wrenching
crease
squabble
tantalizing
facets
architecture
moonstone
dismay
becoming
hued
peers
poised
caw

## Part 2: Sharing the Wonder

1. At first this story seems like a fairly ordinary description of an unhappy birthday party. When does it change into something else? How does the writer let us know we should start to expect incredible things to happen?

2. How many different *settings* are there in "Flora's Birthday Party"?
3. To understand this story, it is important to know that everything and everyone at the yew-alley birthday party represents something or someone at Flora's birthday party. For example, Sticky might represent Serena, the little girl at Flora's party who acts sticky-sweet. If you like to solve puzzles, see if you can figure out what each of the following characters and objects represent:

   Quills
   Hooks
   Angles
   Slime
   The Queen
   The beautiful apartment with its friendly furniture
   Hunt the Pincushion
   The colored glass block buildings
   The looking glasses
4. How did Flora's experience in the yew alley teach her something valuable?

SETTING: Settings include the time and place where a story happens. Descriptions of the settings help the reader to imagine each scene in the story. A setting may be described in a simple way or in great detail. Writers use settings to create different moods or feelings and to make the story seem more real or exciting. Sometimes the setting is a symbol for an idea.

## Part 3: Finding Your Own Faerie Gold

**Brainstorm:** What makes a birthday party fun? What makes it awful? Try to remember the birthday parties you've attended (your own or someone else's). Which one did you enjoy most? Which one did you enjoy least? How could a dream or a visit from a fairy have changed the way you felt about the party?

**Go for the Gold!** (Choose one.)

- Write a story in which you describe an unhappy party. The story should begin, like Flora's, in the real world and then move to a fantasy world where fantastic things happen. Be sure to describe the *setting* where each part of the story takes place.
- Pretend you are Flora and you are writing in your diary at the end of your birthday. What would you write?
- Draw one of the *settings* in Flora's incredible dream. Try to make it as much like the story description as you can.

Chapter 12

# A LOST PARADISE

by Andrew Lang

## Part 1: Unlocking Word Treasures

*Rewrite the following phrases in your own words.*

more and more frequent
as if you were in paradise

this was needless
attended to properly
in that tureen
outside the palace
wreaths of forget-me-nots
lined with satin
after a pause
stooped down to peep
to all appearance

## Part 2: Sharing the Wonder

1. What did you learn about the charcoal-burner and his wife from their *dialogue*?
2. Why did the charcoal-burner's wife blame their troubles on "the curiosity of old mother Eve"? (Hint: Read Genesis 3.)
3. In what other ways is this story like the Old Testament story of Eve? (Hint: Genesis 2–3)
4. What are some examples of *irony* in "A Lost Paradise"?

DIALOGUE: When characters in a drama or in a story talk to one another, their conversation is called dialogue. The dialogue can:

- move the action along,
- show us the personality of the speakers,
- reveal the speakers' thoughts and beliefs.

In some stories, the character may say one thing and mean the opposite, or the reader may realize that even though a character means what he says, the opposite of what he is saying is true. This kind of clash in meaning is called *irony*.

Writers listen carefully to people talking in order to learn how to write lifelike dialogue. They also try to balance dialogue with descriptions and action so that we feel as if we can hear, see, and feel what is happening.

## Part 3: Finding Your Own Faerie Gold

**Brainstorm:** Do you think the coal-burner and his wife learned anything from their experience? If so, what did they learn? How would they feel about being made to leave the King's paradise? How might what they learned have changed their lives? What would they tell their children and grandchildren about their lost paradise? What would they say in reply to the last paragraph in this story?

Go for the Gold! (Choose one.)

- Make a cartoon strip that retells the story of "A Lost Paradise." You'll have to make the dialogue between the characters very short in order to put it into word balloons. Plan carefully what you will say in each frame (section) of the cartoon strip, as well as deciding what pictures to put with the words.
- Ask a couple of friends to help you act out the story.
- Write a conversation in which the charcoal-burner gives his son advice about how to deal with a curious wife.
- Write a conversation in which the charcoal-burner's wife talks to her daughter about how curiosity can be good and bad.
- Add another paragraph or two to "The Lost Paradise" in which the charcoal-burner and his wife say something about their grandchildren's confidence that they would not have given in to temptation.

Chapter 13

# JUSTNOWLAND

by Edith Nesbit

## Part 1: Unlocking Word Treasures

*When we want to learn the meanings of words, we usually turn to the dictionary. But to really understand some words and phrases, sometimes we need more than the dictionary. "Justnowland" has some words in it that are best understood by using an encyclopedia and other reference sources. See what you can learn about the following:*

**Foxe's Book of Martyrs:** You can learn more about this famous book and its author, John Foxe, in the encyclopedia or online at http://www.gospelcom.net/chi/GLIMPSEF/Glimpses/glmps121.shtml.

Be sure to learn what these words have to do with martyrs: chains, rack, fiery stake, dungeons, boiling oil, imprisonment.

**Oleographs:** You'll find a definition in the dictionary; but to really understand what an oleograph (also called a chromolithograph) is, try looking in books about the history of printing and book illustration.

**The Bastille:** Look up this infamous prison in the encyclopedia, or you may want to use Encarta software or online service.

**Joan of Arc:** In addition to what you can learn about Joan in an encyclopedia, you'll find many interesting books about this *heroine* (a word you need to know) at your public library.

**Palace life:** "Justnowland" takes readers to a place where there are separate classes of people and rules for how these classes are treated. See what you can learn about: courtiers, court magicians, prime ministers, sovereigns and royalty, field marshals, a king's council, tradesmen, nursemaids, and the poor.

## Part 2: Sharing the Wonder

1. What did Elsie and the dragon have in common?
2. The woman who was paid to take care of Elsie thought that to teach the girl obedience she must break her spirit. The crows of Justnowland had tried in this same way to tame the dragon. Did it work on the dragon? Would it work on Elsie? Is there a better way? (Hint: Ephesians 6:4; Colossians 3:21; Galatians 6:1)
3. The crows of Justnowland learned an important lesson. What was it? (Hint: Matthew 20:25-28; Galatians 5:13-15)
4. There are some similarities between "Justnowland" and *A Little Princess* by Frances Hodgson Burnett. If you have read *A Little Princess*, see how many things you can find that are similar in the two stories.
5. What is the *theme* of "Justnowland"?

THEME: The main idea of a story is called its theme. We find the theme by looking for a repeated idea or a common denominator between different parts of the story. Writers can show a theme through characters, events, and story settings. For example, after reading and thinking about a book like *Stuart Little* by E. B. White, readers might decide that its main theme is learning how to be the person God created you to be and to belong, even when you're very different from your family and friends.

## Part 3: Finding Your Own Faerie Gold

**Brainstorm:** If Elsie made a second visit to Justnowland, what might happen? How do you think things might have changed there? What new adventures could she have? Would Perdona be an important character? What might have happened to the dragon?

**Go for the Gold!** Imagine that you have produced a movie version of "Justnowland." It was a huge success, and now it's time to make a sequel. Write a one-page summary of what will happen in your new movie titled *Return to Justnowland.*

**Chapter 14**

# THE CONCEITED APPLE-BRANCH

by Hans Christian Andersen

## Part 1: Unlocking Word Treasures

*Here are some words from the story to add to your vocabulary treasure chest. If you don't know their meanings, look them up in a dictionary.*

| | | |
|---|---|---|
| conceited | abundance | hedge |
| delicate | nobleman | countess |
| emblem | parasol | lofty |
| transparent | pomp | spared |
| herb | nosegay | paving |
| bough | pity | innocence |
| wreath | garland | blunt |

| | | |
|---|---|---|
| chemist | realms | eternity |
| opinion | draft | cautiously |
| construction | appearance | blush |

## Part 2: Sharing the Wonder

1. Jesus told a *parable* about a man who had a lot in common with the apple branch in this story. Read the parable in Luke 18:9-14. How are the Pharisee and the branch alike?
2. What is the difference between conceit and confidence?
3. Can you put the lesson of the sunbeam into a sentence of your own?
4. Find the place in "The Conceited Apple Branch" where Hans Christian Andersen borrowed some words from Acts 17:28.

PARABLE: A short and often simple story that illustrates a moral or religious truth. Jesus often used parables to teach His followers. (See Matthew 13.) Other examples of parables are Aesop's Fables and Dr. Seuss's *Yertle the Turtle*.

## Part 3: Finding Your Own Faerie Gold

**Brainstorm:** If this story were about animals instead of plants, what creature might be like the apple branch? What creature might be like the dandelion? What could replace the sunbeam as a teacher to the animals?

**Go for the Gold!** Use the story of "The Conceited Apple Branch" as your model for writing your own parable. Choose animals to replace the plants mentioned in the story.

Chapter 15

# A HANDFUL OF CLAY

by Henry Van Dyke

## Part 1: Unlocking Word Treasures

*Here are some words to add to your vocabulary treasure chest. Write a word that means close to the same thing for each one of them.*

| | | |
|---|---|---|
| virtues | descend | caress |
| unison | murmur | fetters |
| lofty | tribulation | distress |
| trample | trough | consolation |
| molded | revolved | kindle |
| penetrating | brood | endure |
| confidence | fashioned | furnace |
| impartial | consummation | destined |
| sullen | discontent | thrust |
| disgrace | rubbish | greenhouse |
| glorious | vessel | scepter |

## Part 2: Sharing the Wonder

1. Was there anything wrong with the clay's dream of becoming something great? What was its *motivation*?
2. What mistake did the clay make? How did its attitude change by the end of the story?

3. There are several places in the Bible where people are compared to clay and God is compared to a potter. Read the following Bible verses: Isaiah 29:16; 64:8; Job 10:9; Romans 9:20–21. After reading these Scriptures, think and talk about how they might have inspired the author of "A Handful of Clay" in writing his story.
4. What might the lilies blooming in the clay pot be a symbol of? (Hint: 2 Corinthians 4:7)

MOTIVATION: An important question to ask about story characters is "why do they do what they do?" What is the reason behind their actions? What do they want? What do they fear? What do they value most? Sometimes the writer tells us exactly what a character's motives are, but more often we have to look at several parts of the story to tell. There are some important things to remember about judging motives: 1. what comes out of a character's mouth tells a lot about what is in his heart, 2. actions speak even louder than words, and 3. only God can know all that causes someone's words and actions. (Matt. 12:33–35; 1 John 3:16–18; Prov. 5:21; Heb. 4:12–13)

## Part 3: Finding Your Own Faerie Gold

**Brainstorm:** What are some things that become special because of what they contain or what they are made into? What might each one of these things think about itself? Would it think it was special, or would it feel ordinary or even ugly?

**Go for the Gold!** (Choose one.)

Write a story similar to "A Handful of Clay," but instead of clay, make it about:

- A woven basket
- A sack of flour
- A cardboard box
- A piece of metal
- A sheet of paper

## Chapter 16

# THE NIGHTINGALE

by Hans Christian Andersen

### Part 1: Unlocking Word Treasures

*After you are sure you know the meaning of each word below, divide the words up into three groups: 1. nouns, 2. verbs, 3. adjectives and adverbs.*

| | | |
|---|---|---|
| emperor | priceless | porcelain |
| brittle | majestic | nightingale |
| scholars | circulated | accounts |
| rank | ventured | corridors |
| invention | imperial | trample |
| courtiers | chaplain | esteemed |
| enchanted | perch | lackey |
| chambermaid | parcel | mechanical |
| artificial | compared | clockwork |

| duet | bandmaster | plumage |
|---|---|---|
| forefinger | lacking | banished |
| physician | respects | relieve |
| divine | lullaby | bough |

## Part 2: Sharing the Wonder

1. Why did everyone except the Emperor and his courtiers seem to know about the Nightingale?
2. In what way is this story a little like the story called "The Emperor's New Clothes"?
3. Can you think of some modern examples of how people behave like the Emperor and his court? Do they ever think that something artificial is better than the real thing?

COMPARING & CONTRASTING: When we point out the similarities (comparisons) and differences (contrasts) between two things, ideas, or people, we are comparing and contrasting. For example, you might choose to compare and contrast two fairy tale characters, like Snow White and Sleeping Beauty. There are some things these two have in common, but there are ways in which they are quite different.

## Part 3: Finding Your Own Faerie Gold

**Brainstorm:** What made the real nightingale special? What made the mechanical nightingale special? How would you decide which one was most valuable? Would different people value the two birds differently?

**Go for the Gold!** (Choose one.)

- Make believe that you are in charge of the complaint

department at a store. Your store wants you to politely encourage people to keep the things they've purchased rather than returning them for a refund. Write a report to the store manager about the following:

- Your first customer of the day brings in a live nightingale in a cage and wants her money back. Write down her complaints, a description of the item being returned, and what you said to the customer.
- Later a customer brings in a mechanical nightingale and wants his money back. Write down his complaints, a description of the item being returned, and what you said to the customer.

- Go to the library and look for the magazine called *Consumer Reports*. Study an issue of the magazine to see how it reviews the good and bad points of various things. Then create your own "Consumer Report" in which you compare the value of a live nightingale to a mechanical nightingale.
- Write a one- or two-page composition in which you compare and contrast the courtiers with the common people in "The Nightingale."

## Chapter 17

# A CHRISTMAS STAR

by Katherine Pyle

### Part 1: Unlocking Word Treasures

*Check the meaning of these words in the dictionary. Then write twelve sentences, using one of the words in each sentence.*

| entry | speck | clung |
|---|---|---|
| evergreen | counter | dazzled |
| clasped | ornaments | worthwhile |
| neglected | anxious | particular |

## Part 2: Sharing the Wonder

- How can you tell that the author of "The Christmas Star" expects her readers to know the story of the Star of Bethlehem?
- Mother Moon didn't explain to the little star what the Wonder Entry was. What do you think it was?
- Have you ever had something that was as special to you as the star was to the little boy? Describe it.
- By thinking carefully about this story and its details, make the following *inferences:*
    - In what century did this story probably take place?
    - Where might the story have taken place?
    - What happened to the boy at the end of the story?

INFERENCE: Sometimes writers give us enough facts for us to know things with certainty. They may tell us exactly when and where a story takes place, what the characters are like, and what the results of story events are. Many times, though, writers give us clues about these things and leave us to figure out what these clues probably mean. The opinions we reach are called *inferences*. For example, the story titled "The Emperor's New Clothes" does not tell us that the emperor is stupid or unfit for his position; but by the end of the story we can make the inference that he is both, based on what he does.

## Part 3: Finding Your Own Faerie Gold

**Brainstorm:** What is your favorite Christmas ornament or decoration? What thoughts and feelings might it have? Where might it have come from before you got it? What adventures might it go on? What does it do in between holidays? What will happen to it when it grows old?

**Go for the Gold!** Write your own Christmas story about a special ornament that is born, lives, and dies like a human being. You can make your story somewhat like "A Christmas Star." Or, for more ideas about the secret life of toys, read *The Velveteen Rabbit* by Margery Williams, *Big Susan* by Elizabeth Orton Jones, *Noelle of the Nutcracker* by Jan Brett, or *The Steadfast Tin Soldier* by Hans Christian Andersen.

**Chapter 18**

# THE COMING OF THE KING

by Laura E. Richards

## Part 1: Unlocking Word Treasures

*Part of knowing what a word means is being able to picture the thing it represents. When you can picture it and how it is used, then you can find the right words to describe it.*

1. Describe the use of these tools mentioned in the story: hoe, rake, wheelbarrow.
2. Describe the appearance of these plants in the story: rushes, garlands of oak leaves, pine tassels, marigold buds.

3. Describe an old barrel and an old cape used in the story to make a throne.

## Part 2: Sharing the Wonder

1. After the children worked on the playground, what did they realize they wanted to do?
2. What made the traveler say "good," then "better," and finally "best" to the children?
3. What does the Bible say about the way the children treated the traveler? (Hint: Matthew 25:31–40; Hebrews 13:1–2)
4. Find the *simile* in this story. Does it give you a clue about who the traveler was?

SIMILE: An expression that compares two things that are mostly unalike by using the connecting words *as, like, than,* or *seems.* Here are some examples of similes from the Bible:

> "The kingdom of heaven is like a treasure hidden in a field." (Matthew 13:44)
>
> "The path of the just is like the first gleam of dawn...." (Proverbs 4:18)
>
> "As the deer pants for streams of water, so my soul pants for you, O God." (Psalm 42:1)

Have fun learning more about similes by checking out Norton Juster's *As Silly as Bee's Knees, As Busy as Bees* and *As: A Surfeit of Similes.*

## Part 3: Finding Your Own Faerie Gold

**Brainstorm:** Do you think the traveler who stopped at the playground was a poor man? An angel? Or the King in disguise? What reasons might the King have had for traveling in the clothes of an ordinary man? If it was the King, why didn't he tell the children who he was before he left? How would this story be different if the traveler told it?

**Go for the Gold!** (Choose one.)

- Pretend that you are the traveler who stopped at the playground. The day is over and you are writing in your diary. What would you say about your experience at the playground?
- Make a diorama of the children's playground. Here are two places on the Internet where you can learn more about making dioramas: http://www.princetonol.com/groups/iad/lessons/elem/elem28.html; http://www.abcteach.com/babysit/projects/dioramas.htm

**Chapter 19**

# THE CASTLE

by George MacDonald

## Part 1: Unlocking Word Treasures

*Chose a partner to help you find the meanings of the following words in the dictionary, and then:*

- put a check mark by the ones that have to do with buildings,

- put a star by the ones that have to do with nature,
- put a heart by the ones that have to do with people,
- put an X by the ones that have to do with ideas and beliefs.

*Do any of these words fit in more than one category?*

| | | |
|---|---|---|
| noble | presumed | architecture |
| suites | legends | foundations |
| accuracy | perforated | honeycombed |
| conviction | voids | inaccessible |
| accustomed | tradition | chaos |
| tyranny | stately | stern |
| heartily | proportion | persuaded |
| intention | expectation | vault |
| pursued | hospitality | improper |
| gaudy | platform | billows |
| torrents | girdle | pillars |
| arches | brooded | dread |
| astronomy | astrology | compass |
| probability | prophecy | primrose |
| orchid | molded | dignified |

## Part 2: Sharing the Wonder

1. Why do you think George MacDonald spent so much time describing the castle before he said anything about the people who lived there?
2. Would you like to have lived in this mysterious castle? As the oldest brother? As one of the other children?

3. What other stories have you heard or read in which a brother is disliked and his brothers and/or sisters try to get rid of him? (Here's a classic in the Bible: Genesis 37.)
4. Why did the brothers and sisters feel and act so differently after the storm?
5. If you like to look for hidden meanings in stories, think about how "The Castle" is an allegory about our Father God, Jesus Christ, and God's children.

CHARACTERS: The people in stories are called characters. Through their thoughts, actions, and descriptions we get the feeling that we know them as individuals. Some characters have major parts in the story, while others may only make brief appearances. As the writer creates the story, she thinks about how to make each character unique—in appearance, speech, interests, attitudes, and personality. When you recall the stories you love best, you're likely to find that you love them most for their unforgettable characters. The art of creating and developing characters is called *characterization*.

## Part 3: Finding Your Own Faerie Gold

**Brainstorm:** Think about how the writers helped us understand what each *character* was like. What can you determine about the father and each of his children by looking closely at their descriptions, speech, and actions?

Go for the Gold!

- Make a character report card. Decide what character qualities you think are most important in everyone and create a report card on which you can mark the story characters' grades. Then give each of the main characters in "The Castle" the grades you think they deserve based on how much or how little they showed each character quality in the first part of the story. Then make a second report card for the characters based on the attitudes and behavior they showed by the end of the story.

Chapter 20

# THE LOVELIEST ROSE IN THE WORLD

by Hans Christian Andersen

## Part 1: Unlocking Word Treasures

*Once you're sure of the definitions for the following words, make a word-matching puzzle to try on a friend. There should be a numbered definition for the player to match to each of the words below.*

| | | |
|---|---|---|
| hedge | scented | passage |
| ceiling | fragrance | worthy |
| class | splendor | coffin |
| obtain | refreshed | dreary |
| renew | vows | baptism |

## Part 2: Sharing the Wonder

1. What kinds of roses did people think were the loveliest? How was the last rose better than them all?
2. If the wise man knew what the loveliest rose was,

why didn't he bring it to the queen?

3. What book did the queen's son read to her from? (Hint: You'll find the words he read in John 15:13.)
4. How did the loveliest rose bring the queen assurance that she would never die? (Hint: John 3:16; John 11:25.)

IMAGERY: There are five ways we can experience something—through our sense of smell, taste, touch, sight, or hearing. When we are reading, we are only seeing words on a page. To help us feel as if we are experiencing the story with our other senses, the writer uses detailed descriptions. These descriptions or mental pictures are called *imagery*. Here is an example of imagery from *The Adventures of Pinocchio*:

> Pinocchio was able to catch a glimpse of the sky filled with stars, as he looked up through the open jaws of his new home [inside the Shark].
>
> "The time has come for us to escape," he whispered, turning to his father. "The Shark is fast asleep. The sea is calm and the night is as bright as day. Follow me closely, dear Father, and we shall soon be saved."
>
> No sooner said than done. They climbed up the throat of the monster till they came to that immense open mouth. There they had to walk on tiptoes, for if they tickled the Shark's long tongue he might awaken—and where would they be then? The tongue was so wide and so long that it looked like a country road. The two fugitives were just about to dive into the sea when the Shark sneezed very suddenly and, as he sneezed, he gave Pinocchio and Geppetto such a jolt that they found themselves thrown on their backs and dashed once more and very unceremoniously into the stomach of the monster.
>
> To make matters worse, the candle went out and father and son were left in the dark.

## Part 3: Finding Your Own Faerie Gold

**Brainstorm:** Look for the different ways Hans Christian Andersen used *imagery* to make his story more vivid. What pictures do you see in your mind as you read each paragraph? Which ones speak the most to your five senses? What kinds of words besides adjectives and adverbs are an important part of these word pictures?

**Go for the Gold!** (Choose one.)

- Make a poster illustrating all the kinds of roses (plants and humans) that are mentioned in this story. Give the most important place to "the loveliest rose in the world."
- Write a cinquain (pronounced *sin kane*) based on this story. A cinquain is a poem with a certain number of syllables in each of its five lines. The first line has two syllables; the second line, four; the third line, six; the fourth line, eight; and the fifth line, two. The words in it do not rhyme.

  Here is an example:

  The rose  
  fragrant  
  blooming, climbing, blushing,  
  encircling my heart with love,  
  one rose.
- Design an emblem or logo based on this story. The great Reformation leader Martin Luther's personal emblem (coat of arms) was a rose. He put a red heart in the white rose's center and a black cross in the center of the heart. The background was blue to represent heaven. And the motto that went with this emblem was: "The word of the Lord abides forever." You may want to create a motto to go with your emblem, too.

Chapter 21

# ROBIN REDBREAST

by Selma Lagerlof

## Part 1: Unlocking Word Treasures

*See if you can find a word or short phrase that means close to the same thing as each word below. If you cannot, write the word's definition as shown in the dictionary.*

| | | |
|---|---|---|
| paradise | goldfinch | meadow |
| impatient | poisonous | pursue |
| cricket | palm | destined |
| entirely | cooed | pleading |
| pheasant | countless | ornaments |
| dawned | brier | forbears |
| twitter | mourn | beautify |
| downy | valor | victory |
| courageously | sought | procession |
| spears | executioner | iron-clad |
| crucified | shrieks | brow |
| glance | pity | torture |
| forehead | beak | compassion |
| vanish | | |

## Part 2: Sharing the Wonder

1. What two historical events are mentioned in this legend?

2. Is there a difference between using your imagination to make up a story based on something in the Bible and adding to the Bible?
3. How did the robin expect to get his red breast? What character quality did he show that won him his red breast?
4. Sometimes, like the robin, we can feel dull and wish for more colorful lives. What does the legend of "Robin Redbreast" tell us about how we can become more attractive people? (Hint: Matthew 5:16; Colossians 3:12; 1 Peter 3:3–4, 8–9.)

LEGEND: A story that comes down from the distant past and is considered historical by many people even though its facts cannot be proven. The first legends were stories about religious figures (gods, saints, and heroes) and places. Some legends are about make-believe characters who are sometimes mistakenly thought of as real historical figures, such as King Arthur or the Flying Dutchman.

## Part 3: Finding Your Own Faerie Gold

**Brainstorm:** Do you know any other *legends* about how certain creatures received the appearance or abilities they have? Would you like to try making up your own legend? You can use "Robin Redbreast" as your example. What historical events, people, or places would you put in your story? Would the story have a happy, sad, or funny ending?

**Go for the Gold!** (Choose one.)

Tell a legend about:

- How the goldfish became gold.
- How the zebra got its stripes.

- How the dog got its bark.
- How the goat got its beard.
- How the mockingbird got its song.
- How the leopard got its spots.

Other legends you may enjoy: *The Tale of Three Trees* by Angela Elwell Hunt, *Little Rose of Sharon* by Nan Gurley, *Sanji's Seed* by B. J. Reinhard, *The Merchant and the Thief* by Ravi Zacharias, and *The Crippled Lamb* by Max Lucado